a jazzy christmas

ISBN 978-1-4234-9567-3

 Music Sales America

EXCLUSIVELY DISTRIBUTED BY

 HAL•LEONARD® CORPORATION
7777 W. BLUEMOUND RD. P.O. BOX 13819 MILWAUKEE, WI 53213

Visit Hal Leonard Online at
www.halleonard.com

Contents

6   Away In A Manger

8   Deck The Halls

10   Ding Dong Merrily On High

12   God Rest Ye Merry, Gentlemen

14   Hark! The Herald Angels Sing

16   The Holly And The Ivy

18   Silent Night

20   We Three Kings Of Orient Are

22   We Wish You A Merry Christmas

Performance Notes

Away In A Manger

A gentle jazz waltz, this tune contains reasonably long phrases. Equip yourself for these by taking deep breaths before the start of each phrase, enabling a strong sense of legato which will help the melody float over the accompaniment of the rhythm section. Also try playing the melody-line eighth notes with a very slight hint of swing.

Deck The Halls

It is of utmost importance that you keep to a steady tempo throughout this piece and do not succumb to the temptation to push ahead of the beat. This is particularly the case at the first entry of the melody in bar 9 when, given the absence of the piano, it is essential to lock in with the walking bass line. A similarly good sense of ensemble is also required in bars 17–20 when both you and the piano are playing the melody. Play out more during the solo section at bar 33 but remember to bring your volume back down at bar 49.

Ding Dong Merrily On High

This tune will benefit from a laid-back, almost throwaway sense of swing. Again, there are some long phrases and you should try playing each of the descending passages (bars 11–16, 19–24 and later, bars 59–64 and 67–72) in one breath. Good ensemble playing is also important in these bars as the piano joins you in playing the melody. At bar 35 it is in fact the piano that states the melody so think of yourself as providing an accompanying counter-melody at this point.

God Rest Ye Merry, Gentlemen

Work towards creating a marked contrast between the legato sections of this piece (such as bars 25–31) and the snappy, rhythmic passages that sandwich them. A similarly striking contrast should be created between the smooth half notes and jazzy eighth note movement in the solo section at bar 61. Pay careful attention to placing your notes with the rhythm section at bar 9 and once again, don't rush.

Hark! The Herald Angels Sing

This simple, gentle arrangement provides the perfect opportunity to display both controlled legato playing and increased emotion and expression. As in 'Away In A Manger', the classical, almost hymn-like melody should glide over the jazzy rhythm section, creating an effortless sense of contrast.

The Holly And The Ivy

Another jazz waltz to be played in a relaxed, almost lazy style. The eighth notes in this arrangement should be swung except in a few instances (such as bars 10–11 and 18–19). The extended solo section (bars 25–56) affords the opportunity to slowly build intensity, but ensure you return to the original relaxed feel when the melody is restated at bar 57, and play the last seven bars with a reflective feel.

Silent Night

Resist the temptation to push ahead of the beat in this slow, thoughtful arrangement, especially during the solo section, to avoid giving the music any unwanted edge. Take deep breaths to see you through the long legato phrases and keep the dynamics fairly muted.

We Three Kings Of Orient Are

Keep the rhythms tight in this up-tempo arrangement, and give the accented notes a little extra bite to create a sense of anticipation. Practice the tricky "corners" in bars 45–60 slowly, without the backing track, increasing the speed as your fingers become more comfortable with the eighth note movement. Listen to the demonstration at bar 77 to inspire your own ad-libbed solo.

We Wish You A Merry Christmas

Another traditional carol given the fast-jazz treatment, this jaunty arrangement moves between a feeling of 'in 2' and 'in 4'. Listen carefully to the backing track at bar 27 in order to ground yourself at the start of the solo section when the piano is tacet. You can afford to add a dash of humor to your performance at the very end.

Clarinet in B♭

Away In A Manger

Words: Traditional
Music by William Kirkpatrick

Easy Swing (Straight Eighths)

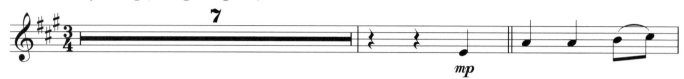

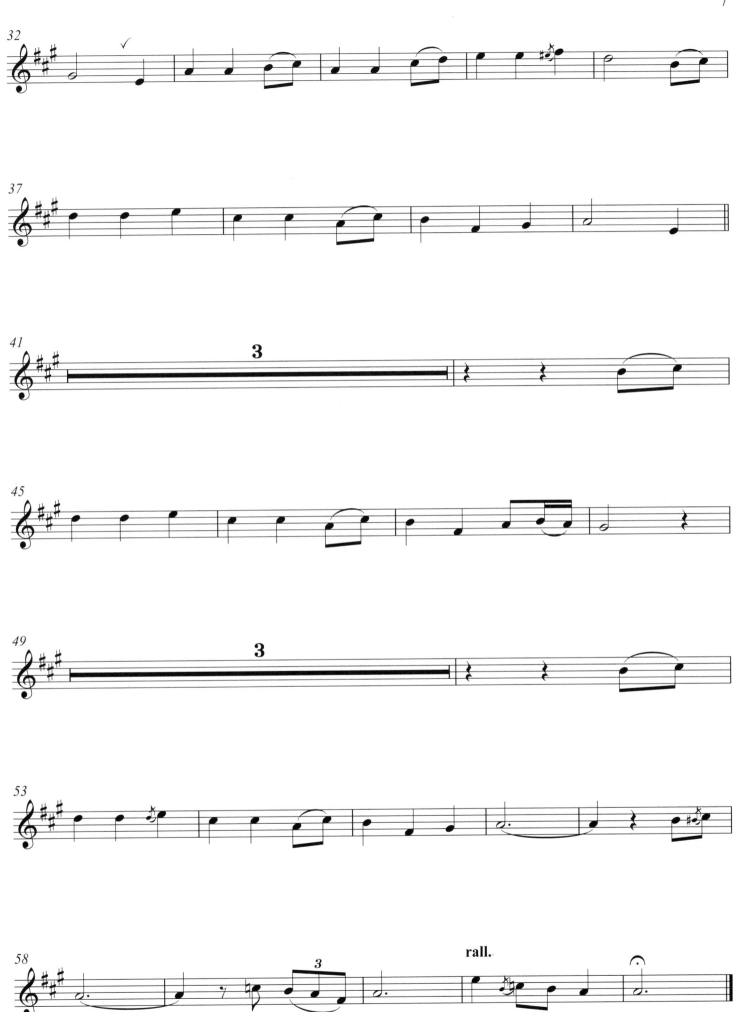

Clarinet in B♭

Deck The Halls

Traditional

Clarinet in B♭

Ding Dong Merrily On High

Words by George Woodward
Music: Traditional

Clarinet in B♭

God Rest Ye Merry, Gentlemen

Traditional

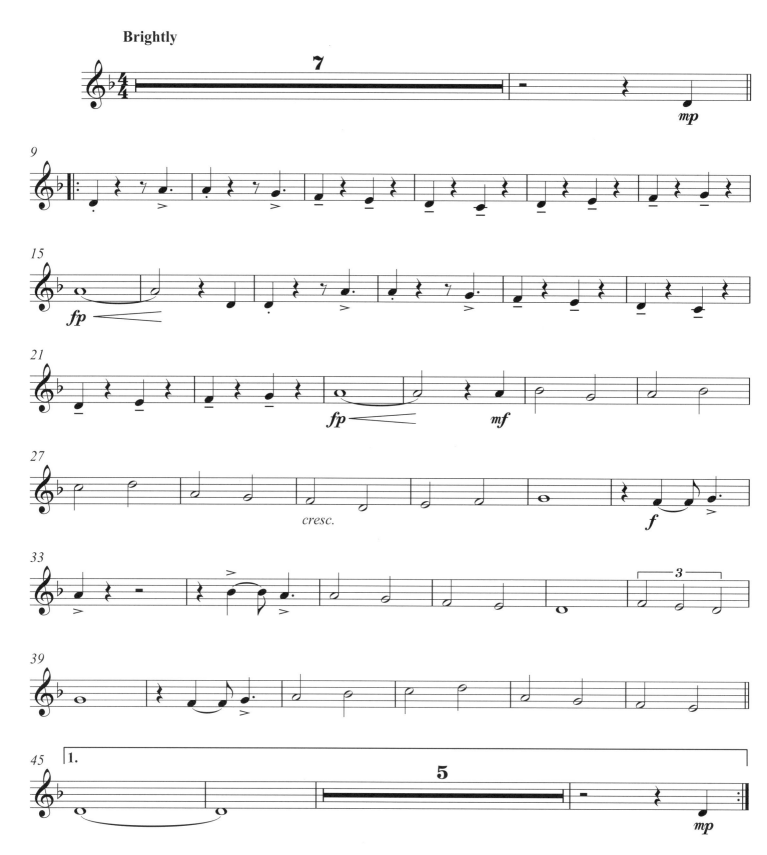

Clarinet in B♭

Hark! The Herald Angels Sing

Words by Charles Wesley
Music: Traditional

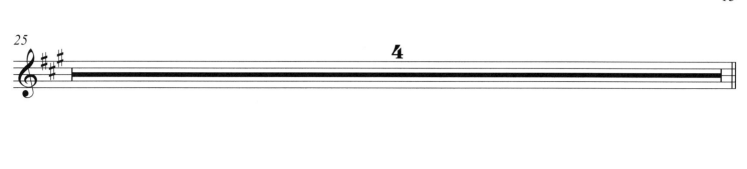

Clarinet in B♭

The Holly And The Ivy

Traditional

Clarinet in B♭

Silent Night

Words by Joseph Mohr
Music by Franz Gruber

Clarinet in B♭

We Three Kings Of Orient Are

Words & Music by John Henry Hopkins

21

Clarinet in B♭

We Wish You A Merry Christmas

Traditional

CD Track Listing

1 **Tuning Notes**

Demonstration Tracks

2 **Away In A Manger**
(Traditional/Kirkpatrick)
Dorsey Brothers Music Limited.

3 **Deck The Halls**
(Traditional)
Dorsey Brothers Music Limited.

4 **Ding Dong Merrily On High**
(Traditional/Woodward)
Dorsey Brothers Music Limited

5 **God Rest Ye Merry, Gentlemen**
(Traditional)
Dorsey Brothers Music Limited.

6 **Hark! The Herald Angels Sing**
(Wesley/Traditional)
Dorsey Brothers Music Limited.

7 **The Holly And The Ivy**
(Traditional)
Dorsey Brothers Music Limited.

8 **Silent Night**
(Mohr/Gruber)
Dorsey Brothers Music Limited.

9 **We Three Kings Of Orient Are**
(Hopkins)
Dorsey Brothers Music Limited.

10 **We Wish You A Merry Christmas**
(Traditional)
Dorsey Brothers Music Limited.

Backing Tracks

11 **Away In A Manger**

12 **Deck The Halls**

13 **Ding Dong Merrily On High**

14 **God Rest Ye Merry, Gentlemen**

15 **Hark! The Herald Angels Sing**

16 **The Holly And The Ivy**

17 **Silent Night**

18 **We Three Kings Of Orient Are**

19 **We Wish You A Merry Christmas**

CD Mixed & Mastered - Jonas Persson
Keyboards - Paul Honey
Bass - Don Richardson
Drums - Chris Baron
Alto Saxophone - Howard McGill